Street Corner Philosopher

By: Prince Isaac

<u>Contents</u>

Negus…   Pgs 1-8

Fear/Doubt repudiates faith… Pgs 9-12

Capitalism: The Best Remedy for Black America, and the Truth about Income Inequality between Blacks & Whites… Pgs 13-20

Don't Forget About Those Alive Whom Law Enforcement Have Murdered!!... Pgs 21-24

Is saying: "I hate Niggers" the same as saying: "I Love my Niggas"…   Pgs 25-29

Black Rage…   Pgs 30-35

In Loving Memory
Of
Robert "IG" De Jesus

NEGUS

Negus- Come now, let us analyze man.

Barone- Must we make such an endeavor, man is not as sublime as the universe, let us analyze it, certainly it's much more intriguing than flawed beings. And therein the universe we will find an intricate system functioning in harmony while man can't find comity with thy neighbor.

Negus- You underestimate man's extraordinary advancement in civilization. I concede he's totally flawed, but this is the corollary of freewill. It is freewill that makes him imperfect. However, freewill is that which makes him sublime, more so than what we call the universe. Yes, in space where a variety of celestial bodies exist, there appears to be forceful energy flowing and operating in tranquilly. This design is surely intriguing and draws one's imagination into awe, but man has been left to his own volition unlike our animated objects floating in space.

Barone- Is energy not conscious? Where conscious lies freewill must also, right?

Negus- No! There are material beings conscious yet are without freewill- angels, animals and possibly other beings out there in other galaxies we presume exist. The grand architecture created far as we know just man with the blessing and curse of freewill. His ability to either follow a course The Grand Architecture ordained or one he disdained, this man can choose to be subservient to his creator or his own trivia imaginings.

Barone- It seems man has become supercilious, with his endowed freedom of choose, some have deduced from flawed reasoning The Grand Architecture doesn't even exist, how foolish and arrogant he is why must we subject ourselves to analyzing this ungrateful, unworthy Being.

Negus- We can't place all man in such light for a many exercise their freewill rightfully, or at least strive to, you must understand man has a task that is not easily accomplished.

Barone- How can one not be obedient to their creator? How difficult could it be to follow his laws and commands? They enjoy his life but shun the one whom gave them life, like the disobedient child. They don't honor the woman's who womb they were conceived in nor the man who's seed was deposited in the womb, no wonder the magnificent one is disregarded by the creation he installed with immeasurable freedom, they are sons and daughters of the evil one.

Negus- Some, not all. Do you not understand why the world is in the condition it's in?

Barone- Of course I do, man rather use his free choice for his own selfishness, instead of collective environment.

Negus- Your answer lacks profundity, you clearly don't understand why man's world is full of selfishness and all that derives from it.

Barone- I most certainly do understand! The all merciful is giving them a blessing no other being can lay claim to.

(Continued...)

This blessing has served only to increase man's ego, so much so they even think some of them are

more superior than others based upon pigmentation. This thing called ego, a self destructive artificial quality, leading man to division and wars.

Negus- Ah, division! If man was not divided how can he love his enemy?

Barone- You talk as if division is beneficial for man. Division has led them to conquer one another. They can love thy neighbor without division. Love doesn't divide but unite, where there is love God's corporal is there in the mist.

Negus- Yes! Love, a uniting force that reaches its highest manifestation when two or more come together to advance one another's spirit, wellbeing and station in life. Man couldn't appreciate love if they all were without volition. It is freewill that makes love cogent. Do you not understand why God destroyed the tower of Babel?

Barone- Not beyond what has been related, if there is more to it please enlighten your striving pupil.

Negus- Recall man had one language, advancing themselves collectively, building a grand city. Collectively nothing would be withheld from them; how can their freewill be tested if they faced no hard choices, if all were righteous what would separate man from Angels? So the all knowing confused their language and scattered them across the face of the earth. Here we find man's initial division, an act done by the wise one. If man can't communicate with one another, they can't build anything together, if they can't build together they can't advance their world. Would it not have been easy to love their neighbor whom works hand in hand with them in securing life's essentials? Neighbor, refers to stranger; will one choice to love or shun a stranger. Man can only know God through love, so choosing to love thy enemy or neighbor when one can choose not to, is not just obeying God's command but brings forth tangible attributes of God.

Barone- Do you mean to say God purposely divided man in order for them to reconcile?

(Continued...)

Why would such a loving God do such a thing, being the all wise he must have known that bloodshed and mischief would befall them.

Negus- That which he knows, we know not. But we cannot ever blame God for man's bloodshed and mischief, man chooses conditions they come under. If the almighty is present in man's life, bloodshed and mischief is absent. Love, an entity The Supreme Being endowed man with so that man can remain close to him yet willingly. Actualization and materialization of love can't be without hatred. Hatred wouldn't exist without division; man's cognizance of love wouldn't be appreciated, in addition, the principal of darkness will have dominion over man whom doesn't know the power of love.

Barone- How does man bring love into material body?

Negus- He began with loving his creator, by loving his creator he naturally extends this love to others. Albeit the almighty has many attributes, none are detestable, none can ever be man, however, possess multifarious

(Continued...) Page 7

personalities ranging from munificent to abominable; now imagine one who displays traits of evilness, can a righteous man love him? The man embodied with darkness knows no love, but those filled with light knows love and demonstrates it.

Look at the beauty, he who wallows in principalities governed by The Nefarious One, can enter into light being resolute in their pursuit. Light corresponds to truth which can only be found in love's corporal. When one walks in light, he exhibits love to those walking with him as well as those whom walk in darkness.

Barone- Love then, is the entity that can unite man more significant; it doesn't just heed the command it brings The All Powerful One directly into their realm. I have come to see man as a complicated unique being, inherent with the most superb qualities, with the ability to be an image of the most high. He of all creation is blessed with the complex yet exhilarating freewill that's extant even for those whom choose to ignore he who out of his hands shaped and molded them in his image!

Negus- Just think, the one and only God purposely created a being without innate submission to him, oh how loving and merciful he is; the king of kings who's subjects genuflect before him due to self imposed compulsion!

Barone- Yes, He is the embodiment of love; man can also be. When he imitates God's love, hatred and strife cease to exist! Teacher, can I deduce that the tower of Babel wasn't destroyed for positive reasons?

Negus- You can! The all wise wanted man's freewill to be fully actualized, especially with regards to love. Think how painfully onerous it is for the man who's kin is brutally taken by another man; he who is bereaved of their kin must still love thy neighbor. By cleaving man, he was putting man's freewill to the ultimate test, and those whom love thy neighbor and enemy as they love themselves, is reflecting the image of the true and living God!

Fear/Doubt Repudiates Faith

"I say to you, if you have faith and do not doubt...If you say to this mountain, 'Be removed and be cast into the sea,' it will be done." These are the instructions Jesus gave the world. Surely this sagacious man couldn't possibly think a mere mortal man could cast a mountain into the sea based off faith alone, of course not. But would the Christ give such an instruction without having a reason to know this can indeed be materialized with Faith as small as a mustard seed?

Let us examine the mountain spoken of. This mountain is the high daunting challenges we face in life, thus the reason we say things like "mountain of debt," "mountain of trouble," "mountain of ailments," etc. All of these mountains of challenges are the mountain Jesus tells us can be cast into the sea through Faith. Essentially faith can remove the "mountain of debt," and "mountain of adversity." But for a vast majority of people of faith these mountains remain firmly fixed in their path. Their faith is actually null and void due to lingering Fear/Doubt.

Where there is fear or doubt, faith has no residence, for fear and faith are polar opposites that can never co-exist in comity. Where we find fear/doubt and faith in the heart and mind, there we have a double minded man. Such a man can never cast mountains aside, for "he who doubts is like a wave of the sea driven and tossed by the wind... he is a double minded man unstable in all his ways." So when battling life's myriad challenges, how can one do so with both doubt and faith? This is nothing more than a tumultuous mind and troubled heart, which only brings more adversity. If you think challenges are part of the normal course of universal operation, then your life will encounter such disharmony. But by stripping away the fetters of fear and doubt, and putting on the cloak of unyielding faith, you can then walk thru life vanquishing any mountain in your path to righteousness and prosperity.

What other than steel Faith empowered Jesus to go onto the mountain top with the devil, and not be tempted by his lofty offerings?

(Continued…)

Indeed "It is only the Evil one that suggests to you the Fear of his votaries: Be ye not afraid of them, but fear ME if ye have Faith." Both the Bible and Qur'an declare God says to fear him and him alone. Fear of God is why Jesus didn't fear the devil; he knew to fear the devil meant no faith in God the father, and that "those who reject faith and belie our signs, they shall be companions of the fire; they shall abide therein."

If you look at your finances, then say about your debt. "There's no way I'll ever get out of debt. But God will make a way." Are you not being double minded? You are invalidating your faith in God by uttering: you'll never get out of debt. If you feel you need a new environment to live and work in, yet packing up and going into the unknown, you simply can't do due to fear, but merely have some faith God will get you a new home and job can't nor won't happen. Your fear is smothering your faith.

"What does it profit my brethren, if someone says he has faith but does not have works? Can faith save him?" I think not!

(Continued...) *Pg 12*

Faith must be employed with works, which is the striving for Righteousness followed by assiduously striving to see that which ye seeks materialized with faith always at the forefront, unswerving!

It is said "whoever submits his whole self to God and is a doer of good, he will get his reward with his lord; on such shall be no fear, nor shall ye grieve." Righteousness/Faith Repudiates Fear and doubt and arms one with superior weapons, capable of bringing down any mountain. Faith with works propels one to the top of the mountain as well, once there give thanks to God, then reach down to help those still struggling to remove their mountains. So it's my hope "that you do not become sluggish but imitate those who through faith and patience inherit the promises."

Capitalism: The Best Remedy for Black America, and the Truth about Income Inequality between Blacks & Whites.

"Only in America" are the words often shouted by the great boxing promoter Don King. I personally can't recall ever seeing or hearing Mr. King campaign for any particular political candidate or party. But I do vividly remember his mantra "Only in America," and the American flag somewhere emblazoned on his attire. It is not arduous to grasp, understand and emulate his love for America, notwithstanding her ugly past and atrocious acts toward his ancestors. America- despite her past, present and future flaws which is to be expected some man is at the helm of her institutions, he himself being inherently flawed- is exceptional. When juxtapose with any country, past or present, America stands superlatively above all. This lofty position she rightfully holds has little to do with the citizenry. She's one of a kind because of her founding documents (Declaration of Independence, 13 Colonies Constitution and Federal Constitution) are saturated

(Continued...)

with liberty for man and a government beholden to its citizens.

    The men whom composed these unique documents had the benefit of seeing what worked and didn't, from old emperors, kingdoms, etc…ostensibly they extracted the best of those things from those old "countries" and properly disregarded the bad. Unfortunately the countries of old didn't provide much guidance on individual liberty, which these men felt were the pinnacle of not having their nascent country come to ruin in time past as happened to those of the past. After "itching in stone" that America would be a constitutional republic, a clearer picture began emerging with respect to how commerce would be conducted, although the bulk of commercial activity was agriculture. Since freedom's her bedrock, her citizens were positioned to trade in commerce without government hindering their commercial activity.

    Liberty of the people fostered bartering into capitalism.

(Continued...)

Without freedom there's no capitalism; which is the ability of an individual to take their product or service to the free market, thereafter be compensated for such. That's capitalism in a nutshell. America's commercial industries are driven by private individuals not government, which is suppose to place unburdensome regulations on industries so that it doesn't run amuck. Capitalism also gives the individual sole control over their financial affairs; moreover it takes one from rags to riches if they apply themselves. Anyone of sound mind and body has the power to become opulent thru capitalism. Take Mr. King for example, he came from a poverty stricken and criminal past yet managed to capitalize off his skills of speaking, marketing and promoting to rise above poverty and criminal conduct.

Let me provide another example of capitalism at its core; my aunt Sonya, who doesn't hold any college degree, always held a job but still felt a void financially, though she was able to provide food, shelter and clothing for herself and two daughters.

(Continued...)

One of her greatest talents is doing hair, so she began working at a Hair Salon. For years she saved money; with minimal help she has been able to get a small store front property which she turned into: Sonya's Sea Salon. Thanks to liberty she was able to capitalize off her gift to do superb hair and make a business out of it. This is capitalism!

Another example of capitalism, a guy in my neighborhood use to cut hair in his mother's basement, because he was\is good at what he does he had an abundance of clientele, so much so he was able to generate enough revenue to open a six chair Barbershop. Several years later he now owns a few Barbershops. Neither he nor my aunt are of abnormalities. Blacks across the country can likewise capitalize off their abilities to rise above poverty. Of course there will be obstacles, setbacks and discouragement, but discipline, unyielding resolve, and most importantly prayer will serve to remove those things.

(Continued...) *Pg 17*

Capitalism allows the individual to advance their station in life no matter what seen and unseen forces try preventing him or her. If blacks began fostering their talent, or even hobbies, or a trade learned to the point they can proffer it to the free market, this will begin dissipating black poverty. Even for those who wish not to be entrepreneurs, capitalism creates jobs for those whom wish to simply get by without fretting about the next meal and other life essentials.

There are institutions in America racially bias, resulting in unequal treatment; however, capitalism is an equalizer. Think otherwise? Think about this, you have a woman making $50 grand a year, with some disposable income she can buy shares of a Public traded company just as a billionaire can, obviously the latter will have the means to buy much more than the woman, but she has access to tap into the potential wealth of the market. Capitalism! This provides equal opportunity for all, which brings me to the truth of income inequality between blacks and whites.

First it's important to understand that income inequality is inherent in any civilized society whether capitalism, communism, or socialism. In a capitalist society income inequality is a given. Everyone doesn't want Warren Buffet money, nor does anyone want to be poor. However, what causes the disproportioned inequality of income between blacks and whites is the lack of financial literacy on blacks' behalf. Too many blacks don't have a thorough comprehension when it comes to economics, i.e. capitalism, investing, banking, etc. In the home blacks are not being taught how to balance a checkbook, the stock market, or the free market in general. Consequently blacks' incomes remain immobile.

Whites understand and act on the understanding when it comes to investing, thus the reason their paper-wealth places their income highly above blacks'. A white employee will take advantage of their job's matching 401k, where as a black employee won't.

(Continued...)

A white person will live within their means while a black person would rent a three bedroom house for $1,800 a month, with a $300 car note when they're only bringing in $2,750 home a month. Whites would go to a Dave Ramsey seminar, blacks to a Jay Z concert. Whites get a nice tax return check, buy some shares of Coach while it's trading below $40.00, pay a credit card off, blacks get the same check and go shopping, not even aware that Coach, a public trading company is selling shares for less than $40.00, all they know is Coach has a new bag for $400.00.

This among other things is why income inequality exists between the two. It should be noted that income inequality works both ways. Up and down the Appalachian Mountains, there are white communities worst off than black ones across the country; in terms of income. Is not Don King wealthier than countless whites? Is Beyoncé not wealthier than Ann Coulter and the various T.V. and radio host shows she appears on?

(Continued...) *Pg 20*

There are a number of blacks like whites, who don't astronomical riches, but just want to be able to pay their bills, send their children to college and live comfortably. Capitalism provides a person with the choice of how they wish to live, which is the product of liberty. Since our great country is clothed in liberty of the individual, there will be financial inequalities among the people, because one will reap what the sweat of their brow produce and everyone will not equally produce, nor will everyone wish to equally produce. Liberty allows them to utilize capitalism for the means they wish to achieve regardless of race, gender, or upbringing. Capitalism is an equalizer!

Don't Forget About Those Alive Whom Law Enforcement Have Murdered!!

There are more Eric Garners, Michael Browns, and Sean Bells alive than dead. I'm sure that sentence causes one to scratch their head and say "huh?" Well it's the absolute truth, everyday across this country "minority" men and women are being slaughtered; alas just a few recognize this and attempt to cease the killing that's going on. These killings are not literal, you can say they are the equivalent of death for someone still breathing.

In courtrooms law enforcement officials, police, government agents, district attorneys and assistant ones, U.S. attorneys and assistant ones, are committing perjury among unethical acts that are securing unconstitutional convictions that in turn gets individuals a life sentence, or numbers so high that it essentially equates to life. A life sentence is indeed death for the living.

(Continued...)

If one was to conduct a quick Google search of people released from Prison/death-row, due to having their convictions overturned, you will see that these men and women's convictions were overturned either because DNA proved their innocence, a prosecutor withheld vital exculpatory evidence or a witness lied at the behest of a law enforcement official.

Instead of using bullets or choke holds to snub the life out of young minorities, law enforcement uses another fatal weapon to put them in a grave (Prison) for the living dead; that is the Criminal Justice System, where they face a two-edge sword that causes the odds of finding a judge who doesn't also use the Criminal Justice System as a weapon against minorities, are overwhelmingly low. Most judges get to the bench from the prosecutor's office, so their racial biases carry over with them, though they're supposed to be impartial.

Alas "Lady Justice" plays peek-a-boo, and the scales are never equal when a Minority is at the defense table,

(Continued...) Pg 23

so they are sent far away from home,
warehoused and overseen by people inclined
to be bigots, racist, and outright nefarious.
The living dead must walk among those
with such character traits, while repining for
an opportunity to see home again. But even
where a sliver of hope may engender, they
run into mental anguish, knowing they still
must face that same detective or agent, and
prosecutor back in the pristine courtroom
before the former law enforcement official
donning a robe the color traditionally worm
at funerals. Where the scale is tilted towards
the right side of the courtroom, and ol' Lady
Justice quickly lifts her blindfold to see
whether the person on the left side looks like
a scion of the man who conceived her and
the hand who brought her into creation.
Once she sees they are not of her makers she
gives the guy at the table on the right a wink
and a smile, and a similar gesture to the one
who's supposed to uphold her principles.
Either individually or collectively they
become tyrants; history teaches us that on
the hands of every tyrant is blood, moreover
oppression.

(Continued...)

As the great thinker on law said: where the law ends, tyranny begins (John Lock), I shall advance that another way: when justice is subverted to secure a conviction, it's no longer Justice but becomes injustice, which breeds contempt for the Justice System.

So while people rightfully so protest about the lack of Justice for Eric, Mike, Sean, Tamir and etc… don't forget about those whom law enforcement murdered by using the Criminal Justice System. Though they are breathing they are not living life. Don't forget them for they are tangible examples of a tyrannical system.

Is saying: "I hate Niggers" the same as saying: "I Love my Niggas"

Albeit there's nothing a white person can say or do that can shock my conscious, for his story (history) is inundated with acts of atrocity that only sons of the morning can commit; so me commenting on any word said, or acts done by a white is not because it's so shocking I'm compelled to write or speak upon it. A recent event surrounding the word nigger and whites' usage of it is one of those things I have to give insight on.

I have noticed a pattern in the news whether mainstream, conservative, television or talk radio, whenever a white person is exposed for using the word nigger, immediately after a caravan of people rush to cameras and microphones to opine. A recent event regarding the usage of nigger and whites keeps this pattern on kilter.

(Continued...) *Pg 26*

A YouTube video of white college students chanting racial slurs including nigger and lynching has conservative and liberal whites, and a handful of sycophant blacks contributing these racist usage of nigger to rap music!

Their warped distorted rational is if rappers can saturate their music with nigga, why can't anyone else use it; essentially their view is nigger and nigga is the same. This myopic view has been refuted time after time, but let's remove the often explanation that nigga is a term of endearment and honor not a term of subjugation and belittling. Let's focus on rap and whites briefly.

If whites want to be part of black culture, specifically Hip Hop, then they need be part of the struggle Hip Hop represents, not sit on their lofty ivory towers picking and choosing what Hip Hop terminologies they want to use.

(Continued...) *Pg 27*

Unlike what liberal and conservative whites falsely state, Hip Hop is not filled with Nigga, Bitch, Hoe. In fact the overwhelming majority of Hip Hop is filled with social advocacy and messages of black empowerment. Never do these media people talk about songs like Poison, Ghetto Prisoners, Daughters, and I Can by Nas, nor Public Enemies' "Birth of a Nation" album. Kanye West, who's often in news cycles, has numerous positive songs, yet they rather talk about something he's said or done that they perceive as negative.

Whites whom genuinely enjoy Hip Hop know Hip Hop is not all debauchery; whites whom genuinely like Hip Hop will never chant "I hate niggers" or "lynch niggers," nor will a logical thinking individual contribute a white person's usage of nigger to rappers. Funny thing, those whom have made this absurd comment, tells us things like: "Guns don't kill humans, humans kill humans, a gun is nothing more than a nonliving thing."

(Continued...)

Well what are words other than abstractions of thoughts; what's the difference between rap songs, books, movies, video games? We are told these forms of expression play no role in white boys in school shootings, so why are they saying whites' usage of nigger is due to rappers' usage of nigga?

This really has nothing to do with rap; whites' inability to say nigger in public settings is a blow to his psyche, due to their self-created superiority psyche. Even whites who are not racist engender this artificial superiority thru their subconscious racial biases. Their racial superiority thinking makes the racist white say: "Who the hell is the nigger to tell me I can't say nigger? Imagine how Bill Gates would feel if told he can't use Microsoft products, or Mormons that they can't read the book of Mormon. Being inventors of the word "nigger," whites profoundly feel if they so choose, they should be able to say nigger in any setting and context.

(Continued…) *Pg 29*

More torturing to the racist white is their self-censoring on television and radio, when it comes to stories with "nigger" as the subject, instead they must simply say "the N word." If listened carefully one could hear a fierce desire in them to say nigger instead of "the N word." Even more frustrating is, neither liberals nor conservative whites are why usage of nigger in public is not acceptable and subject to massive backlash; blacks have psychologically beat him in the public square on this front. Think about it, blacks have stripped them of Negro, color and nigger. Yes words are abstract, but they carry power and white superiority is nothing more than feeling and thinking like the all powerful in relation to any other race.

    I can only imagine the casket they will blow when brown people strip them of Richard Nixon's invented "Hispanic" term. Indeed the title is: Is saying "I hate niggers" the same as "I love my niggas," the latter is something rappers frequently state, the former's what racist say, and anyone who thinks it's the same really wants to recapture nigger, in the public square!

Black Rage

Recent events exhibit that the black community is full of rage, frustration and a host of other tumultuous feelings and as usual many people are opining on why; that is "why do they destroy their own community," "why are they rioting," why this why that. These whys are followed by quasi-psychoanalysis of the community by people far removed from the black community. I think it would be fair to say that the white and some blacks whom render their opinion have no substantial contact with black people in urban communities or otherwise, therefore their opinions are nothing more than weightless rhetoric.

In order to offer an opinion that can be taken up to a level of fact that solutions are orientated, or at least a synthesis geared towards a solution, the individual must come down from their lofty towers of abstraction theorizing to tangible contact with the subjects or objects. As one can't look upon any species and give an educated supposition on it without physical examination,

(Continued...)

one can't give an intelligent opinion or synthesis on a group of people without meaningful interaction with those people. So when these individuals bounce around news networks and talk radio, opining on why some blacks are acting in a manner abhorrent to them, it serves no purpose and simply adds fuel to fire because blacks see and hear these inadequate narratives about themselves; further frustrating the process of finding solutions for what's severe problems, this is due to a lack of understanding.

Does this mean a person should have understanding and empathy towards people looting, torching property and committing other acts of ''thuggery,'' absolutely not, however, the country's at large with understanding and empathy can get to the root of black rage, that tend to manifest itself in the base conduct. Why are, particularly young black men full of misdirected rage? A the top of their legitimate grievances is the perpetual injustice they're suffering under the hand of a tyrant judicial system,

(Continued...)

starting with law enforcement's heavy handiness in the community to the courtroom where the constitution and laws are ignored in order to obtain a conviction. Those people, whom opine as I aforementioned, will say police are heavily in these communities due to high crime. Well the crime statistics doesn't born that out. The FBI's uniform crime report- 2012 latest statistic-provide the following numbers of white and blacks charged with crime:

Murder and non-negligent manslaughter: White 4,108, Black 4,203. It should be noted Hispanics are included in the category of black.

Forcible rape:
White 9,027, Black 4,512
Aggravated assault:
White 188,505, Black 102,371
Burglary:
White 147,156, Black 67,554
Larceny theft:
White 677,895, Black 288,025
Motor Vehicle theft:
White 35,251, Black 16,301

Other assaults:
White 606,048, Black 294,678
Weapons, carrying, possession etc:
White 66,909, Black 45,842
Prostitution and commercialized vice:
White 23,172 Black 18,486
Sex offenses (exceptional forcible rape and prostitution):
White 38,063, Black 12,850
Drug abuse violations:
White 801,198, Black 372,914
Offenses against family and children:
White 53,760, Black 25,698

These numbers conspicuously born out crimes are committed by whites astronomically higher than by blacks, so how can it be argued black communities are more crime ridden? What this materializes, even further is that by saturating the community with police who are predominately white, the probability of discrimination easily moves into the realm actualization. Discrimination encompasses a vast amount of things, all of which is unjust, leading to more black rage, and as witnessed in Baltimore, such rage lashes out in destructive ways.

Without understanding and empathy there can be no dialogue, which allows rage to germinate, giving apathy a presence from all people. Apathy is why these individuals destroy their own community. Businesses in these communities are not predominately black so rioters don't recognize these businesses as part of the "hood" though they are in the neighborhood. Notice no homes were burnt or burglarized, yes, businesses destroyed were owned or operated by other minority groups, however, these rioters don't see them as taking a strong hold of their rage so they don't care.

Why the apathy? Majority of business owners in urban communities don't reinvest in those communities; yes they are providing services to the community, are they obligated to reinvest in the community they depend on for business? Of course not, but they should. Take CVS for instance, a multibillion dollar corporation, makes no reinvestment in the community like opening job training centers, community centers, assisting low funded schools, sponsoring constructive activities.

(Continued...) *Pg 35*

Blacks don't see the return of the capital they put into this business 'cause the overwhelming majority of them don't give the community any return, this is why misguided blacks direct their self-imposed and externally produced rage at these businesses. But such callous acts are never right.

Alas, this rage will bring forth more incidents like those in Ferguson, NYC and Baltimore, until blacks are truly given equality and justice in every societal institution; things like police brutality, stop & frisk, planting of evidence, the withholding of exculpatory evidence, purposeful erroneous court rulings that drastically prevent defendants from getting a fair trial must cease. When they do, black rage will cease being destructive!

www.ingramcontent.com/pod-product-compliance
Lightning Source LLC
Chambersburg PA
CBHW071316060426
42444CB00036B/3126